...be returned on ...
...ast date stamped belo...

BEHIND THE SCENES
FILMING A
BLOCKBUSTER

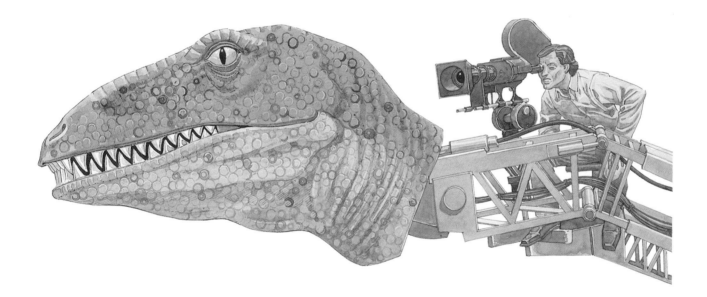

Written by Peter Mellett

Illustrated by John James

Heinemann
LIBRARY

First published in Great Britain by
Heinemann Library, Halley Court,
Jordan Hill, Oxford OX2 8EJ, a division
of Reed Educational and Professional Publishing
Ltd. Heinemann is a registered trademark of Reed
Educational & Professional Publishing Limited.

OXFORD MELBOURNE AUCKLAND
IBADAN JOHANNESBURG BLANTYRE
GABORONE PORTSMOUTH NH (USA) CHICAGO

Editor: Alyson Jones
Art Director: Joanna Hinton-Malivoire
Icons illustrated by: Oxford Illustrators
Cover artwork: Roger Stewart
Printed in Hong Kong

British Library Cataloguing in Publication Data
Mellett, Peter
Filming a blockbuster. - (Behind the scenes)
1.Motion pictures - Production and direction - Juvenile literature
I.Title
791.4'3'0232

ISBN 0 431 02163 5

Acknowledgements
Every effort has been made to contact copyright
holders of any material reproduced in this book.
Any omissions will be rectified in subsequent
printings if notice is given to the Publisher.

Our thanks to Trisha Jenkins from the London
Film and Video Development Agency for her
comments in the preparation of this book.

Any words appearing in the text in bold,
like this, are explained in the Glossary.

CONTENTS

A VISIT TO THE CINEMA

It is sometimes not pleasant to be a movie director. This director is watching the latest blockbuster made by his main rival. Audiences, newspapers and TV commentators think it is marvellous. This director's last movie was successful enough, but not like this one. Sitting next to him is a friend who is a literary agent. Her job is to find good stories for movie companies to use. She nudges his arm: 'I've got an idea...' she whispers.

For this movie a literary agent has read a book that could be turned into a good movie

THE MOVING PICTURE

When you go to the cinema what is actually happening to create the image you are seeing? The 'moving picture' comes from a long strip of **transparent** film. The cinema **projector** shows twenty-four separate pictures every second, each one slightly different from the last. Your eye remembers each picture for a short time after it has disappeared. Your brain joins the images together so you see smooth movement on the screen.

The agent then buys the film rights so that the book can be made into a movie

PROJECTING A PICTURE

Film projectors at the back of the cinema have powerful lamps and **lenses**. They throw an image onto the cinema screen up to 50 metres away. Each picture **frame** on the film is either 35 or 70 millimetres wide and 25 millimetres high. Metal teeth poke through **sprocket holes** in the film to move it along.

film spool

The agent then needs to get a producer and a director interested in the idea of the movie

lens

lamp container

direction of film

loud speakers

screen

holes let sound through

glass beads

WHY IS A CINEMA SCREEN WHITE?

The cinema screen is white so that it reflects as much light as possible. Its surface is coated with millions of tiny glass beads that improve reflection. The sound of the actors' voices comes from loudspeakers behind the screen. The screen is full of tiny holes that let the sound through.

frame divider

film

sound-track

enlargement of film edge

projector

rear speakers

sprocket hole

SURROUNDED BY SOUND

Wherever you sit, the sound is realistic because there are loudspeakers hidden around the cinema. There are four separate sets of loudspeakers, three of them behind the cinema screen. The actors' voices come from the centre speakers, while music and **sound effects** come from left and right. There are extra speakers behind you at the rear of the cinema. They help to make the sound seem all around you wherever you sit.

Finally a screenplay can be commissioned – this is written from the story in the book

SOUND AND LIGHT

The **sound-track** is stored on the projector film. Light shines through two wiggly sound-tracks on the film. The flickering light falls on two **photocells** that make electric signals flow through wires. These signals are decoded to give four separate sound channels that drive the four sets of loudspeakers. The latest sound-tracks are like tiny cut-up pieces of a CD. Each piece is placed in order between the sprocket holes.

PRE-PRODUCTION

The literary agent has talked with a producer at a movie company. He thinks the idea of a time-travel adventure story is great, especially as it will need lots of special effects involving dinosaurs and a flying superhero! The producer is the person in charge of the whole movie-making process from start to finish. The first stage is called pre-production. Producer and director work with a team of about 40 people to plan the movie months before filming starts. The **budget** is $60 million!

THE SCREENWRITERS

Making a movie starts with the screenwriter. The agent has spotted an amazing story in a book. The director also thinks it will make a blockbuster movie. The screenwriter turns the story from the book into a text called the **screenplay**. It is written just like the **script** for a play performed in a theatre. Screenplays are altered many times while a movie is being produced.

VISUALIZING THE MOVIE

The director works with artists who turn the screenplay into a series of drawings called the **storyboard**. Notes are added that give details of **dialogue**, music or special effects. Together, the storyboard and the screenplay help everyone to visualize how each scene will appear and how the action will flow throughout the movie.

The screenplay is finished and artists create the storyboards

LOCATION, LOCATION, LOCATION

The **location** manager travels around looking for suitable places to film each outdoor scene. He contacts the people who own each location, arranges permission for filming and agrees a price. He has to organise closing public streets in towns to traffic during filming.

Outside locations are booked; set design is started; actors are auditioned and hired

A budget is agreed and contracts are signed by the director and the producer

DESIGNERS AT WORK

The production designer is responsible for the overall appearance of the movie. She works with storyboard artists and the director to plan the right visual atmosphere. The **set** designer turns these ideas into instructions about how to build the sets used indoors at the **studio**.

THE WHOLE WORLD'S A STAGE...

The **casting director** hires actors to fill each of the parts in the screenplay. The two main **stars** will cost $5 million each! Actors who want to play the smaller parts come to **auditions**. They show the casting director how they will act their part. She may see hundreds of actors before finally deciding who will get the jobs.

ON LOCATION

Filming outside is called 'shooting on location'. Film **crew** and actors have taken over a whole street. It can take many hours to prepare the actors with make-up and costumes. The director tries to **shoot** as many scenes as possible each day. When all is ready, the director shouts 'Action'. Camera and sound equipment start recording as the actors perform. There may be several **takes** of one scene. It is shot again and again until the director thinks it looks right.

SPECIAL MAKE-UP

How does this actor manage to look like half a dinosaur? The secret is a rubbery latex mask stuck on with special glue. A new mask is used each day, prepared from a model of the actor's head. A rubber skull cap is also pulled on to hide the actor's hair. Layer by layer, the make-up artist builds up the new shape.

NORMAL MAKE-UP

Make-up artists change an actor's face to suit their part. Coloured make-up creams and powders alter age and skin colour. Wigs, false eyelashes, beards and moustaches help each actor to look the same from one day's filming to the next. The completed make-up must look natural under the strong lights often used for filming.

A film crew is assembled: they position the cameras in the best places to film the action

The first scene is filmed; the continuity supervisor makes notes to make sure future scenes match this one

Electric lamps are used to make more light because it is a cloudy day; the director shouts 'Action'

DRESSING UP

The main actors have their clothes and costumes specially made. Often there are several sets of the same outfit. Some are 'distressed' (made to look worn or damaged). A team of people called costumers studied the **script** weeks ago. Using the **studio** wardrobes and rental companies they collected together all the costumes needed by every actor for each scene.

CONTINUITY

The finished movie is made up from scenes filmed at different times. The **continuity** supervisor takes snapshots and writes notes on every scene. Her job is to make sure the scenes match. She advises make-up artists about each actor's appearance and checks that costumes do not change unexpectedly between the scenes.

Make-up artists change the actors face; the costumers collect all the necessary costumes

SUNSHINE ON A RAINY DAY

The sun may hide behind the clouds but filming continues with the help of powerful electric lamps. Huge fans can provide gentle breezes or almost blow the actors over with gale-force winds. If a downpour is needed, it comes from a 'rain cluster' of water sprinklers hanging high above the actors' heads.

MOVIE CAMERAS

Movie cameras are similar to the
projectors used in cinemas. Toothed
wheels and claws move the film through
the camera. A glass **lens** at the front
captures light coming from the scene. The
lens focuses a sharp image onto the film as
it passes through the camera at 24 separate
frames every second. Different sorts of lenses
are used for close-up and
long-distance shots.

*Filming each take continues;
let's get some action shots*

FILMING THE ACTION

In this scene, the camera is fitted to the front
of the car so that it can ride along with the
action. This way the audience will feel the
excitement of the car chase. The camera is
the eye through which the audience sees the
finished movie. The film runs slower
through the camera for this chase
scene and it is also acted slowly for
safety. When the film is played
back at normal speed the
action will speed up.

film holder

lens

lens

viewfinder

three emulsions sensitive to different colours of light

movie camera film

plastic backing

THE FILM

Movie camera film is a long strip of tough plastic about one-fifth of a millimetre thick. It has a coating of chemicals that are sensitive to light. This coat is called the **emulsion** and is just 15 thousandths of a millimetre thick. It has three layers, sensitive to blue, green, and red light.

The film of a full-length feature movie is more than 2.5 km (1.5 miles) long

One minute of filming requires 27 metres (90 feet) of film

COLOUR MIXING

Blue, green, and red are called **primary colours**. Mixing these colours of light in the right proportions will give any other colour. Every colour of light that enters the camera is made up from different mixtures of these three primary colours. The camera film responds to every colour in the scene because it is sensitive to blue, green, and red light.

white light

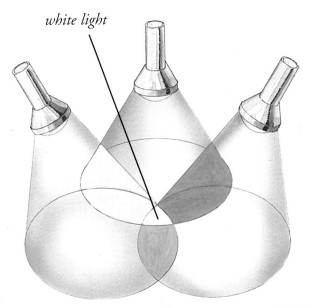

TAKE ONE

At the start of shooting each **take**, the clapper loader snaps the **clapperboard** shut in front of the camera. The clapperboard is a flat piece of wood with a hinged top. Details of each scene are chalked on the front of it. The picture of the clapperboard closing and the noise it makes helps to fit the **sound-track** to the film later on.

RECORDING SOUND

The sound crew use a portable tape recorder. **Shooting** on **location** usually means that sound quality is not good enough for the finished movie. The location recording will be used later to guide the actors in the **studio** as they add (**dub**) their voices to the action.

STUNTS!

Sometimes scenes are far too dangerous for an ordinary actor to perform. The action is done by a specially-trained actor called a stunt double. He or she is made up and dressed to look like the main **star**. Stunts are usually filmed from a distance so the double's face cannot be seen clearly. You will see close-ups of the star later to give the impression that they have performed the action.

compressed air

kicker ramp

pleated rubber skirt

EXPLOSIVE ACTION

A real explosion would kill anyone caught in its blast. Instead the stunt double takes off from a machine called a kicker ramp. It is a flat box with a hinged lid, sealed all around with a pleated rubber skirt. Compressed air blasts into the box and flings the lid up, hurling the actor through the air.

The stunt double puts on an all-in-one flame-proof fire suit over padded body armour

NO BROKEN BONES?

The stunt lasts seconds but takes hours to prepare. Falling at speed from high in the air would normally break bones and cause severe injury. The stunt double has been specially trained and lands on soft crash mats that cushion her fall. Padded body armour safeguards her hips, spine, shoulders and elbows.

A life-like mask of the leading star goes over the suit's underhood

knee pads

elbow pads

padded body armour

STUNTS WITH FIRE

For this stunt the double must also survive flames. The main protection is an all-in-one flameproof fire suit and underhood. Flesh coloured fire gloves protect the double's hands. A life-like mask of the leading star covers the underhood so it looks like the star is performing the action. A copy of the star's costume fits over all these layers.

The stunt double hurtles through the air and lands safely on soft crash mats

Cue explosions; then the kicker ramp

The pyrotechnists have wired up smoke grenades and explosive charges

PYROTECHNICS

Fires, flashes and bangs are organised by experts called **pyrotechnists**. For this explosive stunt they connect electric wires to smoke grenades and small explosive charges. They set these off an instant before firing the kicker ramp. Camera and sound equipment are triggered to start together.

DISAPPEARING FLAMES

A building has caught fire – but the flames disappear at the end of each **shoot**. Gas burners hidden out of sight fire sheets of flames from the windows and doorway. Steel cylinders supply flammable propane gas to the burners. Members of the film **crew** safely control the gas from outside the building.

SET DESIGN

The set designer uses sketches of the set to make a full range of plans. The computer helps him to see the set from any point of view. The set carpenters and decorators also need instructions. They must make the set the right size and shape, and look real.

At the pre-production stage, the production designer plans the set to match the visual feel of the movie

BUILDING A SET

Some scenes for the movie need to be filmed inside the **studio**. This is called **shooting** on **set**. This set has taken many weeks to build. The plans were started during the pre-production stage when the production designer talked with the director and made rough sketches. A set of plans were drawn on computer. Much of the set still looks incomplete but it is finished. Parts that the camera does not see are left bare and undecorated.

The set designer sketches the set; the plans are stored on computer

MAKING A MODEL

Model makers build perfect scale models of each set. These models help the director and technicians to work out where to place cameras and lights. Models are also used for special effects, especially when the director wants the whole scene to burn down or blow up.

WORK BEGINS

Carpenters and scaffolders are the first people to start building the set. The scaffolders put up a framework of metal tubes. Carpenters cut and shape thin sheets of wood and fix them together to make the main structure. Shaped blocks of foamed plastic and sheets of flimsy canvas complete the overall shape of the set.

PROPS

The **props** supervisor has collected together the hundreds of different items needed on the set. Some of the props are part of the set, such as the prehistoric trees which were made specially in the **studio** workshops.

The props supervisor collects all the different items needed for the set

Carpenters and scaffolders make a framework of the set; painters spray it and add fine detail

Model makers make an exact replica of the set; technicians work out where the lights should go

Viewed through the camera the set looks very real!

CREATING AN ILLUSION

Painters use compressed air to spray fine misty jets of paint onto the set. They add fine detail later with small brushes. Viewed from close up, the set looks just like it really is – painted plastic foam and wood. Viewed through the camera with the lighting switched on, it looks completely real and authentic. Like the movie, the set is pure illusion!

GLASS SCREEN

Sometimes things have to be added or removed from a scene. Rather than make a completely new set, things can be added on a large glass screen which is fixed in front of the camera. The futuristic village appears in this scene, but it is only on a screen that covers the upper third of the set.

glass screen

THE SOUND STAGE

This movie **set** has been built inside a huge building called a sound stage. Filming indoors lets you control light and sound – much more than outdoors, 'on **location**'. By mixing lights and colour, the right 'atmosphere' for each scene can be created. Many of the lights are coloured and can shine bright or dim. Some lights hang from rails attached to the ceiling.

spotlight

glass screen

flood-light

clapper loader

LIGHTS

All the light on a sound stage comes from large electric lamps. The ones on a typical sound stage are each as bright as 400 hand torches or 2,000 candles. Flood-lights illuminate large areas. Spotlights project a narrow beam of light that can be seen as a 'spot' of light.

props supervisor

sound crew

ON THE SOUND STAGE

When filming, unwanted noises can be picked up by the microphones. It's easier to control the noise on a sound stage so the **sound-track** for the movie can be recorded at the same time as the scenes on the **set** are filmed.

WHITE LIGHT

White light is actually a mixture of all the colours of the rainbow. A white surface reflects all the colours that make up white light.

A white surface reflects all the colours in white light

When white light falls on a red surface, only the red is reflected. The other colours are absorbed.

Red light is reflected off a red surface

A scene in white light

Red light makes the scene look warmer

CREATING A WARMER SCENE

Electric lamps give out white light. If you slip a sheet of clear red plastic in front of a lamp, only red light shines through. The plastic sheet works as a filter. Red light makes a scene look 'warmer'. It darkens blues (cold colours) and brightens reds (warm colours).

DRESSING THE SET

The set dresser arranges the set to create **atmosphere**. The lights can then brighten the scene or cast dramatic shadows.

GETTING TO GRIPS

A scene can be made more interesting and dramatic by moving the viewpoint. As the actors perform, the camera moves, or **tracks**, around them. In the sound stage some cameras are moved on trolleys on rails. Assistants called **grips** push the trolley along.

director

prop

continuity supervisor

grip

sound crew

It takes about 4 weeks to shoot just 7 minutes of the movie

Scenes are shot together, but not always in the order they will appear

Filming begins on the sound stage; the set will be used for several scenes in the movie

SPECIAL EFFECTS

This movie also requires some 'special effects'. They create the illusion that something extraordinary is happening. This fierce dinosaur is simply an actor inside a very complicated costume. The actor is completely free to move around and use his arms and legs. At the same time, someone out of sight uses radio control to work the life-like face. Eyes, mouth, tongue and skin all move to create a range of facial expressions to make the dinosaur look real.

A TWO-HEADED DINOSAUR

Technicians in the workshop measure the actor carefully. They construct a dinosaur body from soft and flexible latex foam. The technicians make two sorts of head. One contains all the motors and controls for realistic close-up shots of the dinosaur. The other is empty and is used when the dinosaur is in the background of a scene and does not have to be seen up close.

The technicians carefully measure the actor

They construct a dinosaur body from flexible latex foam

MAKING THE HEAD MOVE

The head is covered with a soft rubber mask. Underneath it is a hard plastic skull fitted with moving parts. More than 20 steel cables pull on these parts to make them work. Each cable is attached to an electric motor controlled by radio signals. Using radio control means there are no wires connecting the actor to the **set.** He is completely free to move around.

A MESSY ENDING

This dinosaur is about to meet a gruesome end. **Pyrotechnists** place a small explosive charge inside one of the empty rubber heads. They pack an assortment of apple cores and pieces of foam rubber around the explosive. As a final touch, they add a few small 'blood bags' containing red dye dissolved in sticky corn syrup.

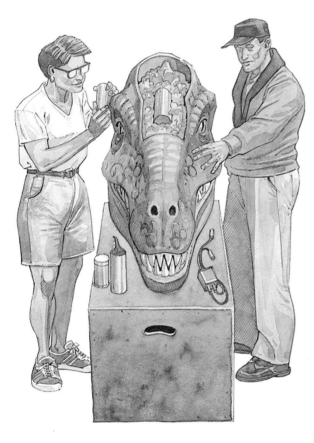

On set it is controlled by radio signals while the actor moves around

The motorized head fits over the top of the actor inside the suit

KER-BANG!

Explosions happen extremely quickly – in just a few thousandths of a second. The camera operator sets the camera to run at high speed. Viewing the film later at normal speed slows down the action. The head contains just enough explosive to burst it open. Too much is dangerous and would not make the finished shot any more dramatic.

LOOK – NO ARMS!

This dinosaur is enormous. Its body would be far too large for one actor to control from the inside. The fearsome head is attached to a metal crane arm that can move in all directions. Steel cables move the eyes, mouth and tongue. The director plans the action carefully so that the crane arm does not appear in the shot.

MORPHING

Smoothly changing one image into another is called **morphing**. Before computers, this used to be done by altering an actor's make-up and filming the face after each make-up change. Now all the computer needs is two images – one of how the actor looks at the start and one of how the director wants him to look at the end. A computer program then smoothly and realistically blends one into the other.

AN IMMENSE STRING OF NUMBERS

Computers use numbers to create these 'digital special effects'. They break each picture down into millions of tiny specks of light called pixels. Each pixel has a set of numbers that describes its position and colour. The computer stores these numbers and then can alter them to create the special effect. This dinosaur is just an immense string of numbers: 10010110 11001001 00100101 10001001 01011......

COMPUTER EFFECTS

The finished scene above depended on camera and computers for its special effects. The person in the back of the car is changing into a dinosaur while another dinosaur is chasing behind. The film **shot on location** had no dinosaur outside the car and just an ordinary actor in the back seat. Computers weave their magic by altering the image on film and by adding a completely new one.

The computer takes the scanned image apart pixel by pixel.

A DINOSAUR THAT CAN SPEAK!

This dinosaur can speak! The computer scans
the actor's face with a beam of light and notes
the position of each part. It links each part to
the corresponding place on the image of the
dinosaur head. When the actor talks, smiles or
frowns, parts of his face alter their position.
The computer moves the dinosaur image
exactly in step so the dinosaur has the same
facial movements as the actor.

In 1981 it took 40 mins to build a computer-generated frame; it now takes one twenty-fourth of a second!

A computer stores 120 million numbers for each frame

THERE'S A DINOSAUR...

The special-effects computer
not only alters images, but it can
add a completely new one. In the
shot filmed on location, there was
just an ordinary actor sat in the back
seat of the car. A team of computer
technicians then entered every **frame**
of this film into the computer.

... IN YOUR CAR!

They add an outline of the dinosaur to each
frame, altering its shape until its movement
looks completely realistic. The computer is
then programmed to fill the outline with an
image of the speaking dinosaur created earlier.
The dinosaur running behind the car has also
been added to the film using computer
special effects.

The actor is filmed hanging from wires in front of a blue screen

He cannot wear blue clothes or they will disappear on the special film

TRICK PHOTOGRAPHY

Some special effects don't need to be created using computers. For this scene the simplest method is to hang the actor from wires in front of a moving background to give the illusion he is flying. Another way is to use a 'travelling **matte**' which is simply a moving mask. This mask creates a clear actor-shaped hole in the background scene. The hole is filled later with a moving image of the actor. These methods can be quicker and just as effective as using a computer.

IT'S BREEZY UP HERE

A wind machine blows air over our hero. It flutters his hair and clothing and completes the illusion that he is rushing through the sky.

HANGING AROUND

The actor is filmed hanging from thin wires in front of a blue screen. The wires are blue and so do not show up against the blue screen. The film in the camera is specially sensitive to blue light.

MAKING A MATTE

Two copies of the film are made. Both are processed so that the blue background becomes clear.

One copy shows the actor in full detail. The second is the matte, or mask. The actor appears as a dark silhouette which on the developed film will appear white or clear.

The matte film and the back-ground film are combined

The hole in the matte film is filled by a moving image of the actor

THE BACKGROUND

This is filmed from a helicopter. The camera operator imagines he is filming someone who is flying. He aims the camera at the place the actor will appear in the finished scene.

The background is filmed from a helicopter

The smoke from the rocket pack is added later using a computer

COMBINING FILMS

The two films – the matte of the actor and the background – are copied together onto a new strip of film. The result is a film of the moving background with a clear hole moving about at its centre. The hole is exactly the same shape as the actor.

THE FINAL FILM

This clear hole needs to be filled in. The background film is now combined with the flying actor film created earlier in which he is shown in detail against a clear background. At last you have your amazing special effect – the hero is flying through the air.

24

THE SOUND-TRACK

At last the filming is completed. Now sound must be added to the movie. Four separate **sound-tracks** need to be created, each going to a different set of speakers in the cinema. This huge desk is called the **mixing console**. It takes in all the different recorded sound inputs, controls their loudness and mixes them together. The sound mixer sits at the console watching a picture of the movie. Her job is to make sure the picture is running in time with the sound.

MAKING MUSIC

Music strongly affects the **atmosphere** of a movie. The musicians play in a recording **studio** where a large tape recorder can separately store the sound from each instrument. The sound mixer later uses the mixing console to bring these recordings together.

The director views all the film from a day's shooting and picks the best takes

MIXING IT TOGETHER

The mixing console can run the film backwards and forwards at any speed. The sound mixer plays the same few seconds of film over and over again, adjusting the sound levels and the timing until the effect is right. Sound and vision must work together.

LOOPING AND DUBBING

Sound quality from **location shoots** is usually rather poor. It is not possible to place microphones close to actors when they are rushing around. Sound is added later by 'looping and dubbing'. The film of each scene repeats in an endless loop. The actors speak the lines again and again until it exactly matches the movement of their lips on the film.

CUSTARD IN A GLOVE

Sometimes **sound effects** need to be added to a movie. What noise do footsteps make in freezing snow? Just like the sound of squeezing custard powder inside a rubber glove. Many sound effects are still best made without the help of modern electronics. This is the simplest way to **synchronize** sound with the film. Every time a foot steps in snow, give the glove a squeeze!

The actors have their own voices dubbed onto parts of the film that were shot on location

Synthesized sounds are created and stored on computer

SYNTHESIZED SOUND

Dinosaur roars, explosions, creepy thudding noises – all these sounds are made by a synthesizer. This electronic device generates electrical signals that match the different sounds. The operator alters each signal until it sounds just right and then stores the noise in a computer. A computer programme selects and calls up each sound when it is needed to fit the film.

Atmospheric music for the sound-track is recorded in a recording studio

ALL TAPED TOGETHER

An ordinary tape cassette contains recording tape just 4 millimetres wide. It holds two stereo sound-tracks. Tape recorders in the studio have tape 20 millimetres wide, with enough room for 24 tracks. These tracks are mixed onto the final sound-track tape which has **sprocket holes** along its sides to match the film.

The sound mixer makes sure the picture is running in time with the sound

20 millimetres

4 millimetres

film sound track

tape cassette

PUTTING IT TOGETHER

The director and editor work closely together to select the film that will make the finished movie. They use a machine called an **editing table**. It is like a movie **projector** that can run at any speed, forwards or backwards. It also plays two sound tapes at once through a speaker. One tape contains the actors' speech and the other is for music or **sound effects**. The editor cuts up and joins together small lengths of film. He **synchronizes** the recording tape so that sound and pictures match.

The sound tapes of the actor's voices and the sound effects are ready

SYNCHRONIZING SOUND AND PICTURES

The **clapperboard** helps to synchronize the sound and the pictures. When played slowly, the recording of the clap from the board sounds like a low growl. The editor lines up this sound with the first **frame** of the film which shows the clapperboard closed.

A BAG OF FILM

Thousands of pieces of film are joined to make up the finished movie. Each piece is coiled up and stored loose in a flat metal can. Each can is carefully labelled. Film waiting for the editing machine hangs from a frame along with the **sound-track** tapes. The ends drop down into a large cotton bag that stops the film from becoming scratched or dirty.

AN EXACT MATCH

A movie is made from four main parts: the picture, the actors' voices, the music, and the **sound effects**. Each of these parts must join together exactly for the movie to make sense. This synchronizer holds the film and three sound tapes. The editor marks them with a wax pencil to show where each tape matches the image of the clapperboard.

JOINING THE FILM

This tool cuts pieces of film accurately along the join between two frames. Pins stick through the **sprocket holes** to hold the film steady. The editor wears cotton gloves to make sure the film is not scratched or marked. Special glue dries rapidly to join the film.

The picture and sound tapes are synchronized; the final film is cut and glued together

The sound is lined up with the sound of the clapperboard at the start of each frame

The director and the editor use the editing table to select the film for the final movie

film cutter

sprocket holes

cotton gloves

The finished movie is shown at a private preview

PREVIEW

The finished movie was first shown at a private preview in front of a special audience. Film experts, marketing staff from the **studio** and ordinary members of the public were invited. They were watching the film for the first time: the director has worked on it for more than a year. Their fresh view helps the director see that several parts need re-editing.

The director re-edits some scenes, the movie is now ready for the gala premiere

TOYS AND T-SHIRTS

The movie cost tens of millions to make. A blockbuster earns hundreds of millions at the cinema box office. As much money again can be made from merchandizing. The producer charges manufacturers who want to make and sell toys, books, games, mugs, and T-shirts linked with the movie. An added bonus is that all these items give the movie free advertising.

THE GALA PREMIERE

Tonight is the first public showing of the movie. The audience includes many movie stars and other celebrities. There are also film **critics** from TV and newspapers. The film will be a blockbuster if millions of people around the world go to see it. People often judge a movie from what the critics write. The director knows the movie has worked out well. But what will everyone else think? Now the lights and TV cameras are pointing at him.

CHARTS AND CHAT SHOWS

To launch a movie, you must have publicity. Weeks ago, the marketing department at the studio swung into action. The **stars**, producer and director appeared on TV chat shows. Radio stations are playing the theme tune which climbs up the music charts. By the day of the premiere, 'media hype' has got thousands of people excited about the movie!

ON GENERAL RELEASE

After the premiere, the main cinemas in large cities receive copies of the movie. It is now 'on general release' and the time has come for the public to give its verdict. There are adverts on national TV and local radio stations and on bill boards. People in smaller towns hear the news and wonder when the movie will be shown at their local cinema.

It's a box-office blockbuster; but will it win an Oscar?

The movie is now on general release; the merchandizing for the movie has gone on sale

A BOX OFFICE BLOCKBUSTER

The director reads reports about the movie in the newspapers. The critics' reviews at the premiere were mixed. 'Half-hearted adventure movie' said one; 'Brilliant special effects' said another. But despite the critics and the director's worst nightmares, millions of people have flocked to see the movie. It has turned out to be the blockbuster of the year!

WILL IT WIN AN OSCAR?

Which was the best film this year? Who was the best director, the best actor and the best actress? Each year there are awards given away such as at the '**Oscar**' ceremony in America and the UK **BAFTA** ceremony. The movie has been nominated for an Oscar which means the director and the stars of the movie have been invited to attend the ceremony. The movie could also win an Oscar for having the best special effects or costumes. They will not know if they have won anything until the results are announced ... tomorrow evening.

GLOSSARY

Atmosphere   the feeling surrounding a film or scene in it

Audition   when an actor has a trial reading of his or her part

BAFTA   the British Academy of Film and Television Awards

Budget   the total amount of money needed to make a film

Casting director   a person who selects and hires actors

Clapperboard   a flat board with a hinged top. Details of each scene are chalked on the clapperboard which is snapped in front of the camera at the start of each **take**

Continuity   making sure film scenes shot out of sequence will join together smoothly and that costumes and props don't change between scenes

Contract   a signed agreement

Crew   all the people connected with the technical side of shooting a movie, including sound engineers and camera operators

Critic   someone who judges films or plays, and writes a review or gives their opinion

Dialogue   a conversation between two or more people

Dubbing   recording an actor's voice after filming a scene so that it fits in time with the film (see **looping**)

Editing   cutting lengths of film and joining them together to make the completed movie

Editing table   a machine that matches together the film and the recorded **sound-tracks** containing speech, music, and sound effects

Emulsion   the layer in a film that is sensitive to light

Frame   one complete picture on a piece of film. Each frame has perforations or **sprocket holes** either side to allow the film to be moved through the projector or film camera

Grip   a person that moves equipment on a set

Lens   a specially shaped piece of glass that bends rays of light

Location   a place away from the studio where filming takes place

Looping   a loop of film that repeatedly shows a scene. Used when **dubbing**, the actors speak the **dialogue** until it is in time with the film

Matte   a mask that covers part of a film to make a space which is filled later with another image

Mixing console   a large desk fitted with volume controls for mixing different sounds together to make the final **sound-track** for the movie

Morphing   using a computer to make one image change smoothly into another. The word comes from 'metamorphosis' which describes a caterpillar changing into a butterfly

Oscar a gold-plated statuette awarded by the Academy of Motion Picture Arts and Sciences for the best achievements in performance and film-making every year

Photocell a device that controls an electrical current depending on the amount of light falling on it

Primary colours the colours, normally red, blue and green, from which all other colours are made

Projector a machine used to send a beam of light which makes an image

Props the different items that may appear on a stage or set, or that may be used by the actors

Pyrotechnist a specially trained person responsible for arranging and setting off dramatic, yet safe, fires and explosions

Rights a legal claim, such as being the only person able to sell a movie abroad

Screenplay the written text on which a movie is based. This can be from an original idea, book or play

Script a copy of every word an actor will say

Set the place where filming takes place

Shoot to film a scene

Silhouette a shadow or outline that is filled in with black

Sound effects sounds, such as horse's hooves, a door closing, and a car's engine, added later to the **sound-track** after filming

Sound-track a narrow strip on the side of a film which carrys information the **projector** uses to make into sound for the movie

Sprocket holes a row of holes along both edges of a film. Toothed wheels poke through the perforations to move the film along

Star a famous actress or actor who has previously appeared in well-known movies

Storyboard a sequence of detailed sketches that outline the flow of action in a movie

Studio the place where a movie is made. It includes the sound stage, dressing rooms, store rooms, workshops and editing rooms

Synchronize to make something match with something else and run at the same time

Take filming of one scene. There may be several takes before a director is satisfied with the filming

Track taking a shot while moving the camera around the scene that is being filmed

Transparent a see-through substance through which light can pass and through which objects can clearly be seen

Viewfinder part of the camera that the camera operator uses to see through to decide what to film

INDEX